NOV 0 1 2013

Under
the
Sea

Jellyfish

Meryl Magby

PowerKiDS press

New York

To Jun Marie Logue, whose mama calls her "Muffin," which also has radial symmetry

Published in 2013 by The Rosen Publishing Group, Inc.
29 East 21st Street, New York, NY 10010

First Edition

Editor: Julia Quinlan
Book Design: Greg Tucker

Photo Credits: Cover, pp. 4, 5 (top, bottom), 6, 7, 9, 12–13, 15, 17, 22 Shutterstock.com; p. 10 Paul Sutherland/National Geographic/Getty Images; p. 11 Jake Nowakowski/Newspix/Getty Images; p. 14 Jeffrey L. Rotman/Peter Arnold/Getty Images; p. 16 Ken Lucas/Visuals Unlimited/Getty Images; pp. 18, 21 © Minden Pictures/SuperStock; p. 19 Robert Arnold/Taxi/Getty Images; p. 20 Norbert Wu/Science Faction Jewels/Getty Images.

Library of Congress Cataloging-in-Publication Data

Magby, Meryl.
Jellyfish / by Meryl Magby. — 1st ed.
   p. cm. — (Under the sea)
 ISBN 978-1-4488-7397-5 (library binding) — ISBN 978-1-4488-7476-7 (pbk.) —
ISBN 978-1-4488-7550-4 (6-pack)
1. Jellyfishes—Juvenile literature. I. Title.
QL377.S4M24 2013
593.5'3—dc23

                        2011045396

Manufactured in China

CPSIA Compliance Information: Batch #WKTS12PK: For Further Information contact Rosen Publishing, New York, New York at 1-800-237-9932

Contents

Simple Swimmers   4

In Every Ocean   6

Jelly Bodies   8

Stinging Tentacles   10

Jellyfish Facts   12

Swarms and Blooms   14

Stages of Life   16

What Do Jellies Eat?   18

Jellyfish Predators   20

Humans and Jellies   22

Glossary   23

Index   24

Websites   24

Jellyfish are among the simplest swimming animals on Earth. They do not have brains, blood, hearts, or bones. In fact, their bodies are more than 95 percent water! They are also some of the oldest animals on Earth. Jellyfish lived in Earth's oceans long before dinosaurs walked the land. They have been around for over 500 million years.

Jellyfish live in all of Earth's oceans. This jellyfish lives in Australia, in the waters around the Great Barrier Reef.

There are many kinds of jellyfish. However, not all animals that we call jellies are true jellyfish. True jellyfish have stingers and bell-shaped bodies. Most also have **tentacles**. They are related to sea anemones, sea whips, and coral.

Top: This species of jellyfish is known as the mauve stinger.
Bottom: This jellyfish is known as a crown jellyfish.

5

In Every Ocean

Jellyfish live in all of Earth's oceans, from the **tropical** waters of the Caribbean Sea to the icy waters of the Arctic Ocean. Different jellyfish live in different ocean **habitats**. Some even live in freshwater. In fact, some jellyfish live in places where no other animals can live.

This is a compass jellyfish. These jellyfish live mostly in the cold waters of the North Sea.

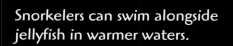

Some **species** of jellyfish live only in one area of the world. Others can live in different places. Jellyfish can be carried long distances by ocean **currents**. An ocean current may carry a group of jellyfish to a new habitat. If there is enough food to eat there, the jellyfish may **colonize** the area.

Jelly Bodies

Jellyfish are **invertebrates**. That means they do not have skeletons. Instead, they have very simple bodies with three layers. The first layer covers the body's surface. The middle layer is made of a jellylike material. The inner layer lines the jellyfish's gut. There is one hole for food to travel in and waste to travel out. Their simple **nervous systems** let them respond to light, smells, and touch.

Jellyfish come in many shapes, sizes, and colors. Scientists have found about 200 species of jellyfish so far. However, they think there may be as many as 2,000 species.

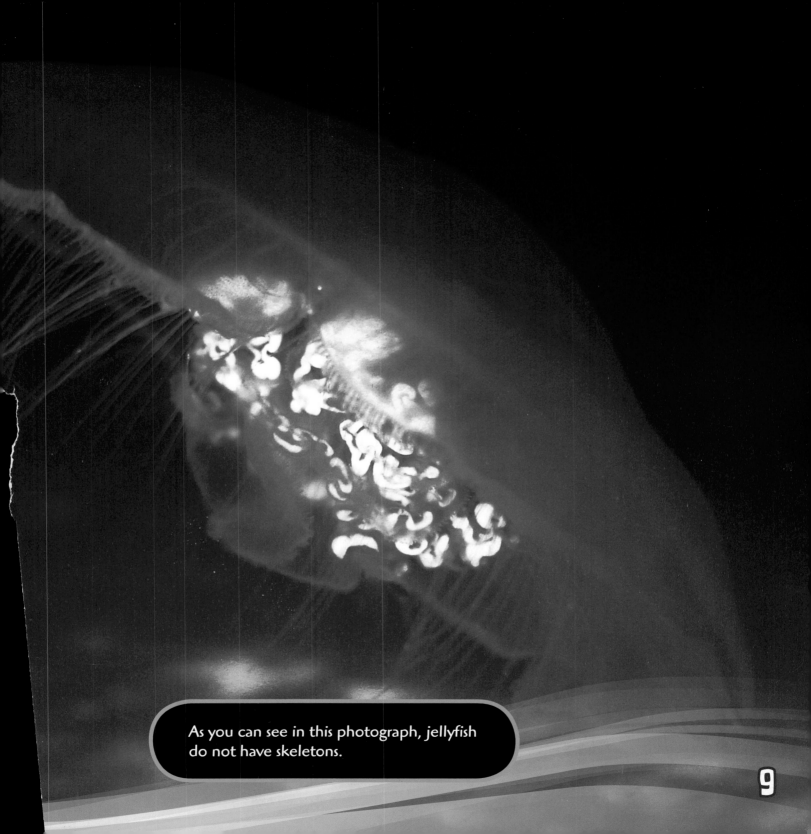

As you can see in this photograph, jellyfish do not have skeletons.

Stinging Tentacles

All true jellyfish sting. Jellyfish have stingers in their tentacles. In each stinger, there is a capsule with a coiled thread inside. When something brushes against the jellyfish's tentacle, this thread quickly uncoils and shoots **venom** into the prey. A jellyfish tentacle may be filled with thousands of stingers.

Box jellyfish stings are very painful. Their tentacles can still sting even after the jellyfish has died.

Irukandji jellyfish are very small and very venomous.

Most jellyfish species are not harmful to humans. However, the stings of some jellyfish species can be very painful and can even cause rashes or cramps. The stings of some jellyfish species, such as the box jellyfish, can be deadly! Most people who are stung by jellyfish are stung in warm or tropical waters.

Jellyfish Facts

1 Many jellyfish live in shallow waters along coastlines. However, some jellyfish may live in waters up to 12,000 feet (3,660 m) deep!

2 Some lion's mane jellyfish have tentacles that are more than 100 feet (30 m) long. This makes this jellyfish species almost as long as the largest animal on Earth, the blue whale!

3 A female jellyfish may release about 45,000 eggs into the ocean in one day.

4 Many jellyfish live in the **polyp** stage of their life cycle for a period that lasts just days. However, some jellyfish may stay in the polyp stage for years or even decades.

5 Jellyfish stingers keep working after a jellyfish has died. This means that dead jellyfish or jellyfish tentacles that have washed ashore can still sting you!

6 A jellyfish's stinger shooting poison into its prey is one of the quickest movements in nature.

7 One species of box jellyfish, the sea wasp, is the most venomous animal in the world. Its sting can kill a person in under 3 minutes.

8 Small fish often live with large spotted jellies. The fish hide from predators inside the spotted jellies' bells.

9 Scientists found a species of hot pink, bell-shaped jellyfish in the Pacific Ocean near Costa Rica. These jellyfish live in extremely hot waters near underwater volcanoes at depths of 8,500 feet (2,590 m).

Swarms and Blooms

Jellyfish cannot easily swim sideways. Instead, they move by being carried by ocean currents. Currents sometimes push large numbers of jellyfish together. This is called a jellyfish swarm.

Jellyfish may also swarm when an ocean habitat has good living conditions. This might mean that there are few predators and lots of food. Other good

These tiny jellyfish, called thimble jellyfish, are swarming in the Caribbean Sea.

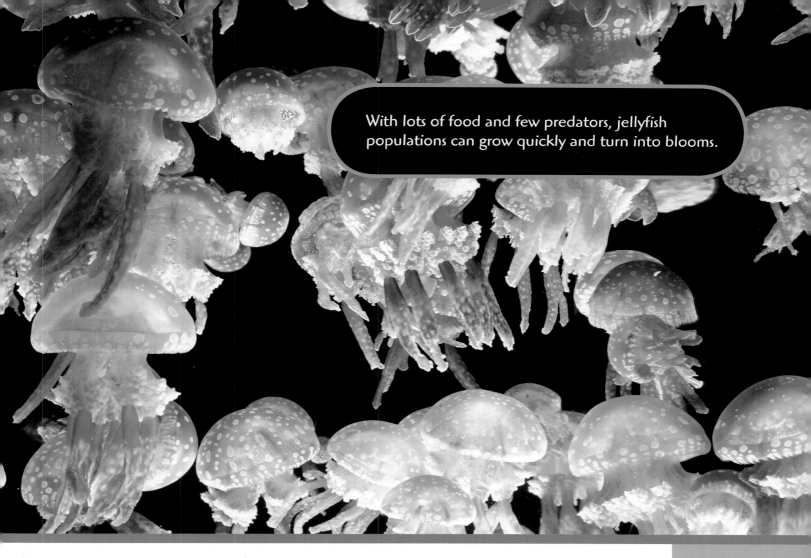

With lots of food and few predators, jellyfish populations can grow quickly and turn into blooms.

conditions could be the right water temperature or amount of salt in the water. When a group of jellyfish **reproduces** more quickly than normal, it is called a jellyfish bloom. When this happens, a large swarm of jellyfish can take over an ocean habitat.

Stages of Life

True jellyfish begin their lives as **larvae**. Larvae float in the water before settling to the ocean floor. There, they attach to something hard and grow into polyps. After a time, the polyps start to get longer. Many young jellyfish form off of each polyp and float away. These jellyfish will grow into adults.

Jellyfish polyps form from larvae and eventually turn into medusae.

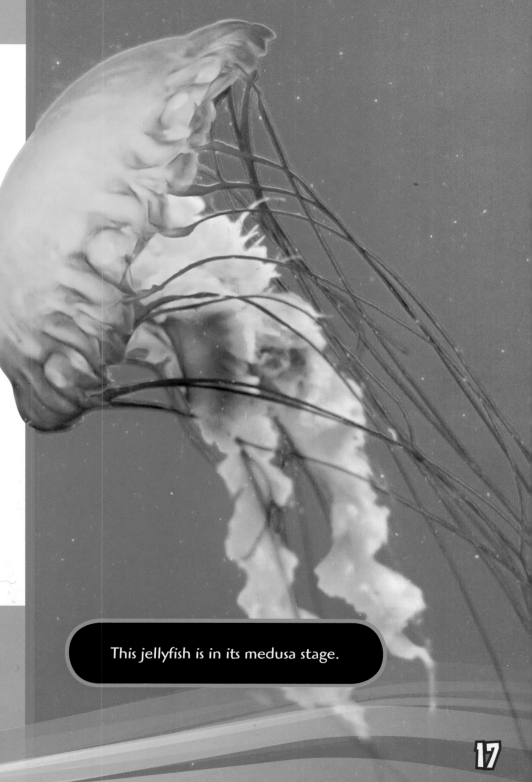

Adult jellyfish are in the medusa stage. Adult female jellyfish release eggs into the water. Male jellyfish then **fertilize** the eggs. The fertilized eggs become larvae.

Comb jellyfish reproduce differently. Each comb jelly makes larvae by itself. These jellyfish form larvae that become adult jellyfish without a polyp stage.

This jellyfish is in its medusa stage.

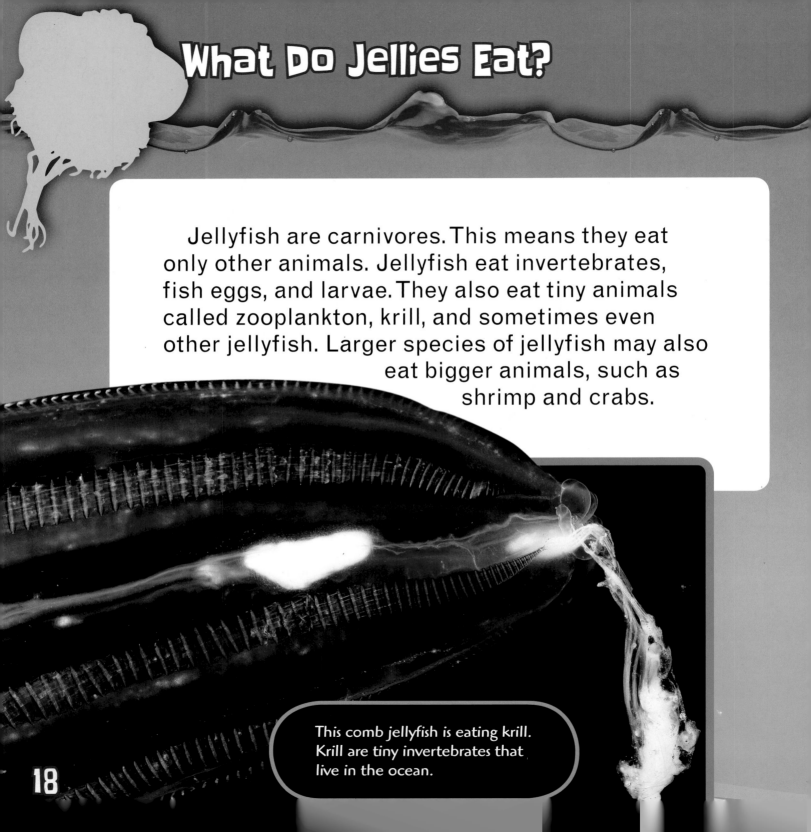

What Do Jellies Eat?

Jellyfish are carnivores. This means they eat only other animals. Jellyfish eat invertebrates, fish eggs, and larvae. They also eat tiny animals called zooplankton, krill, and sometimes even other jellyfish. Larger species of jellyfish may also eat bigger animals, such as shrimp and crabs.

This comb jellyfish is eating krill. Krill are tiny invertebrates that live in the ocean.

Krill are small animals that are related to shrimp and crabs.

Jellyfish do not hunt or attack other animals. Instead, they wait for small animals to brush against the stingers in their tentacles. The sting **paralyzes** or kills the prey. Then, they use body parts called oral arms to move the food to their mouths.

Jellyfish Predators

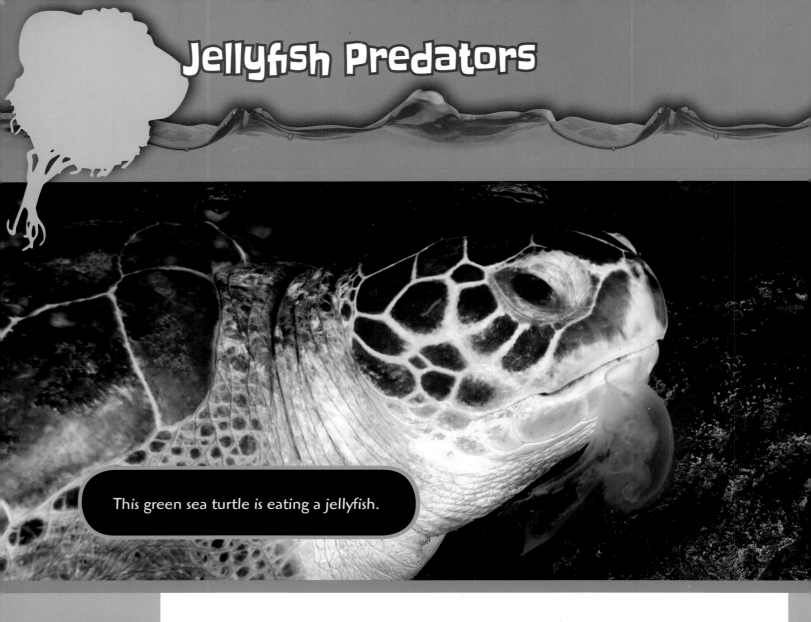

This green sea turtle is eating a jellyfish.

Seabirds, fish, turtles, and other jellyfish eat jellyfish. Their stings do not hurt the animals that eat jellyfish. However, most predators only eat jellyfish larvae and young jellyfish. Adult jellyfish do not have many predators.

People also eat some species of jellyfish! Mushroom and cannonball jellyfish are delicacies, or special foods, in some places. In some Asian countries, pickled or dried jellyfish are very popular.

Jellyfish cannot quickly swim away from predators. However, they can easily hide from predators in plain sight. This is because they are almost see-through. Some jellyfish avoid predators all together and live in places where they have none.

Jellyfish can get stuck in the tentacles of sea anemones and be eaten by them.

Humans and Jellies

Scientists think that jellyfish may be taking over some ocean habitats because of overfishing. When fishermen catch too many of a certain kind of fish, it is called overfishing. With fewer fish, there is more food for jellyfish to eat. Lots of food can cause a jellyfish bloom.

Jellyfish swarms are bad for ocean habitats and people. Sometimes beaches are shut down because jellyfish have stung many people or there are too many jellyfish in the water. Taking care of the environment may help bring jellyfish numbers back to normal!

People must take care of the ocean to prevent harmful jellyfish swarms.

Glossary

colonize (KAH-luh-nyz) To take over a new area.

currents (KUR-ents) Water that flows in one direction.

fertilize (FUR-tuh-lyz) To put male cells inside an egg to produce young.

habitats (HA-buh-tats) The places where animals or plants naturally live.

invertebrates (in-VER-teh-brets) Animals without backbones.

larvae (LAHR-vee) Animals in an early period of life.

nervous systems (NER-vus SIS-tumz) Systems of nerve fibers in people or animals.

paralyzes (PER-uh-lyz-ez) Takes away feeling or movement.

polyp (PAH-lip) The first stage of a jellyfish's life.

reproduces (ree-pruh-DOOS-ez) Produces young.

species (SPEE-sheez) A single kind of living thing. All people are one species.

tentacles (TEN-tih-kulz) Long, thin growths on animals that are used to touch, hold, or move.

tropical (TRAH-puh-kul) Having to do with the warm parts of Earth that are near the equator.

venom (VEH-num) A poison passed by one animal into another through a bite or a sting.

Index

A
Arctic Ocean, 6

B
bodies, 4–5, 8
bones, 4
brains, 4

C
Caribbean Sea, 6
coral, 5
current(s), 7, 14

D
dinosaurs, 4

E
Earth, 4, 12
eggs, 12, 17–18

F
food(s), 7–8, 14, 19, 21–22

G
group, 7, 15

H
habitat(s), 6–7, 14–15, 22
hearts, 4

I
invertebrates, 8, 18

K
kind(s), 5, 22

L
land, 4
larvae, 16–18, 20

N
nervous systems, 8

O
ocean(s), 4, 6, 12–13

P
predators, 13–14, 20–21

R
rashes, 11

S
skeletons, 8
species, 7–8, 11–13, 18, 21
stage, 12, 17
stinger(s), 5, 10, 13, 19
sting(s), 11, 13, 19–20

T
tentacle(s), 5, 10, 12–13, 19

V
venom, 10

W
water(s), 4, 6, 11–13,
     15–17, 22

Websites

Due to the changing nature of Internet links, PowerKids Press has developed an online list of websites related to the subject of this book. This site is updated regularly. Please use this link to access the list: www.powerkidslinks.com/uts/jelly/